Vision is Not Enough

A PROACTIVE APPROACH TO LIVING A FRUITFUL LIFE

Ope Adenuga

TRILOGY CHRISTIAN PUBLISHERS
TUSTIN, CA

Trilogy Christian Publishers
A Wholly Owned Subsidiary of Trinity Broadcasting Network
2442 Michelle Drive
Tustin, CA 92780

Manufactured in the United States of America

10 9 8 7 6 5 4 3 2 1

Library of Congress Cataloging-in-Publication Data is available.

ISBN 978-1-64773-540-1

ISBN 978-1-64773-541-8 (ebook)

Contents

Dedication

This book is dedicated to Yahweh of Israel; God will not share His glory with any man.

To men and women who believe in my vision, and have become part of my story.

Acknowledgements

First, gratitude to the Almighty God for the privilege I have, the love I am enjoying, and the mercy I do not deserve but is bestowed on me.

I want to appreciate Pastor Korede Akindele and his family for providing a platform to serve God and others under his leadership at Redeemed Christian Church of God (Victory International Center). It is indeed a privilege to serve.

My profound gratitude goes to my family, those who believe in my vision when it was a mere dream. These friends see and make time for what many see as an illusion. A big thanks to Mrs. Modupe Adenuga, Mrs. Amma Yeboaa Fredua, and the caregivers that work with me every day to add value to the lives of the vulnerable population that we serve. Thank you for your support.

Special thanks to RCCG (VIC) past and present Sunday school teachers, Minister Aaron Hopewell and Dr. Oyewole Adeyeye, for serving with me in that ministry.

May the Lord remember your labor of love and reward you.

To the eagles that gathered with me every December 31st for family meetings, you have a place in destiny; you cannot afford to fall short of His high expectations.

I would also like to thank those that volunteered their time and talent to proofread the manuscript and work on seminar presentations; my darling Ivie Okieimen and engineer Tosin Adeboye your vision will flourish. You have a place at the top.

The editors and my children, Jemima, Simi, Godsfavor, and Emmanuel—thank you.

To my family at Disciples Commission International Mission fields, many of you taught me how to persevere—thank you.

To my spiritual and familial mentors, Rev Fola Olusanya, Pa Babatunde Abiala, Pastor Ayo Thomas, O.K Adenuga, and Bola Adenuga, thank you for being there in those challenging days—I have learned different attributes from each of you. There is a miracle in people—you are part of God sent in your little way.

Finally, to my siblings, our late parents taught us to be enterprising and face life as a warrior, not as a victim. I am proud of all of you.

Thank you for your time and investment.

Foreword

I am delighted and honored to write a foreword for my friend, Ope Adenuga, who has been a relentless and passionate witness for the cause of Christ. I have known Mr. Ope Adenuga for over eighteen years and watched him live out the principles in this book. He has grown from employee to an employer of labor, at the same time, staying faithful and committed to the success of our ministry!

In this masterpiece, *Vision Is Not Enough*, the author has provided us another tool for navigating through the issues of life successfully and finding true fulfillment in God, even when our vision is challenged. This book was written to help shape our work with God in His purpose and empower us as we all continue to press to attain the purpose on which Christ Himself had laid hold of us. Reading this book, Ope takes us through the process of conceptualizing vision to the actualization and manifestation of vision.

Over the years I have known him, he has taught some of the topics in this book to our Sunday School audience, and testimonials abound from those under his tutelage about how the nuggets shared have been instrumental in their success story to the glory of God.

This book is proof that heavenly visions are real and are to be pursued through prayer, the ministry of the Word, and Godly counsel. It is a call for personal reflection and a must-read for each one of us that will impact our generation and perhaps generations yet unborn. I pray that as you carefully go through this book, you will make a firm commitment to live a life of purpose unto His glory. This inspirational work speaks to every age and everybody that has a desire to lead a life of impact. I am proud of this work; it is easy to read and understand.

In the service of the King,
Pastor Akorede (Kore) Akindele

In his book, the author encourages us to look at "what is in our hand." He uses the example of the widow and the jar of oil that is found in the Old Testament (see 2 Kings 4:1-7). By using what she has, she is able to use a seemingly insignificant item to reverse her situation. With a vision, you can accomplish more. This book helps you to define your vision and encourages the reader to do something meaningful with what you have.

Elias Kanaris
Executive Director of Lifework Leadership, Auckland
Founder of the CEO Global Summit

This book is very inspiring, rekindles hope, and stimulates one's appetite for great accomplishments in life. Yes, having a vision is not enough. Until vision translates into appropriate actions, it is indeed irrelevant. I recommend the book to everyone who desires to live a fruitful life.

Reverend Fola Olusanya
General Overseer, Living Stone Builders Ministries

This new season is one of non-stagnancy, but season of merit, value, and structure. Many authors talk to the readers through how to be "great" or "achieve the impossible." But many overlooked the limitations that prevent a well-learned college professor from achieving what he taught. The "why and how" is hard to figure out. The book, *Vision is Not Enough*, written by Ope Adenuga, takes you on a journey of self-reflective and self-encouraging enrichment. Written from his own experiences, the book takes you through the art of finding your purpose in life. It describes how to get there; what to do when you are "there." It brings self-awareness to finding and pursuing your vision in life for your significance and the stability of the next generations. Varying from different examples of the biblical text to different quotes of inspirational speakers and writers, the book encourages you not to be stagnant but to find out "why you are here" and to pursue it when you have a little glimpse of the answer. Time is precious; time is of the essence, do not waste it if you have it. Many have lost time, and they cannot get it back because it is too late. Losing time is the worst thing we can do to ourselves and those that could have better direction through our vision. *Vision is Not Enough* unravels the essential concepts to living a fruitful life. These pages voyage in-depth and persuasion will leave you blessed, ready to take action, and evolve as the words fill your heart.

Simi Adenuga
Daughter of Ope Adenuga

Overview

It is with great pleasure that I write an overview of this book conceived and nurtured to fruition as a testimony to the author's belief and understanding of these concepts. I will describe the book's content as an inspired work meant to challenge our generation who may have become too comfortable after the Industrial Revolution's great work. This book is a wakeup call to action for all of us at any level of success or misery.

I used the word 'inspired' deliberately in the first paragraph. As the writer stated in his introduction, and like other ideas that he has developed and nursed to fruition in the ensuing pages, seems to be an inspiration born out of revelation as he dug inward while performing his duty in the ministry that God gave him. In the writer's own words, "God will meet you in the place of the work He assigned to you."

This work, or rather treatise, is sufficient to provide the necessary impetus to challenge and cause the willing individual to change the course of their life for the better. The writer made a great attempt to establish the difference between vision and purpose. The nature of this differentiation will enable people who have read books on purposeful living and the importance of purpose to find the missing link in conceptualizing and thus bringing into reality what they have been trying to see. It is worth mentioning here that the concept is developed in a milieu of references, which in themselves are sufficient to show the effort made to make the idea practical.

In the first part of the book, the vision's general concepts and meanings are described to clarify vision as a living entity. The approach appears to challenge individuals to live a productive life with a purpose of excellence not only for the individual but for posterity. In developing the concept of vision and why it is needful, necessary components of a "living vision" was explained. The living vision is woven with the phases of vision development in such a way to encourage the readers to understand the stage at which vision is conceived, birthed, nurtured to fruition.

The second part of the book delved with patience and deliberately into the practicality of the idea of vision, its place in the meaningful living, and how it generates the needed start-up plan for a journey into a successful life. The author showed how vision is not enough with real-life examples and other profound ingredients that must accompany the vision to make it a reality.

The book's practical nature recommends itself to all individuals who need a new perspective on vision. It is also for individuals who need to learn a new dynamic of vision that can fuel and propel that novel idea that has been sidelined for a long time into reality for generations yet unborn.

I wish you happy reading and may the Lord God, who caused this book to be written for such a time as this, meet you at the point of your needs.

Samuel Oyewole Adeyeye, Ph.D., MPH, RD.

Preface

Life provides equal opportunity for all of us that are privileged to be here. We are all born with the same human features and characteristics: one head, two hands, two legs, two ears, two eyes, and the list goes on. We can move, we can grow, and we are all subject to extinction. How we use and deploy these features are different, and so also our outcomes.

In 2019, I was exposed to Exit Realty International brokers/owners training in Ontario, Canada, with some partners. I saw amazing statistics for the first time. The statistics have been around, but I never paid attention. The statistics showed that the wealthiest one percent of American households own forty percent of the country's wealth.[1] I also learned that ten percent of the world's population leads and feeds the remaining ninety percent.[2] While many people got upset about the statistic and planned to write articles and editorials on the evils of a plutocrat, I decided to take as much as I can learn from the seminar.

I developed a wave of anger in me, but it was not towards anyone or any system that deprived me of opportunities. My resentment was directed towards my ignorance as much as I think I know. It propelled personal questions. My questions were: who am I, and what is my place in this world? Why am I here, what are the reasons for my existence other than the rat race that does not take me anywhere, and what can I do to make a difference with this one life? What are the differences between wealthy households and the poor? Both the rich and the poor inhale oxygen and exhale carbon dioxide. Why the dichotomy?

Without searching too hard, I discovered my answer—*vision* separates the two. One has a sustainable vision they are living for; the others do not. One perceives the world as a risky and insecure habitation and will chase security all their life. Even when they are secure, the fear of insecurity will still taunt them. The others see life as an exploration domain and swim in the ocean of risks; they have defeated their fear of the unknown and invariably living in freedom. One understands the importance of the economy in social dominance; the others do not. One understands production; the others enjoy consumption. The poor buy the products of the rich and make them more productive.

Vision is the hallmark that will determine your real worth and net worth. Many people have their visions shaped by their family beliefs, religious philosophy, society, or cultural norms but will never think outside the box.

In 2002, I was hired to fulfill the vision of Wellstar Health System. I was happy and celebrated with my friends about my dream job. I had job security. I could pay my bills, support my family, and flex muscles among my friends because I had a job with one of the best places to work in Atlanta with about ten thousand employees. The happiness soon waned in the face of constant practice expectations.

I have a desire for self-expression, soon it dawned on me that I was made for something more than a job; that was the beginning of my quest for and desire to live my vision. I have been pursuing my dreams and aspirations—the total of my vision. Amid this pursuit, I discovered that having a vision is not enough.

Vision affects an individual's outcome, and a nation can be bankrupt for lack of vision or aborted vision. The global pandemics that have overtaken the world and poised to send the best economy in the world to a recession with over twenty-four thousand job losses and unemployment in double digits in a few weeks is staggering. Can you imagine that the best jobs that seem secure are not truly secured? Many employees have been furlough while the vision bearers will take ownership of their businesses until the tides turn.

America, as a world leader, had a vision of a looming pandemic that may cripple the world. Two former presidents, George W. Bush in 2005 and Barack Obama in 2014, spoke concisely about the impending pandemic that may stalemate the global economy. They visualized and had the mental image of the perceived devastation, but I suppose that they thought vision was enough. Despite America's intelligence, influence, sophistication, and advancement, we do not seem to be better than other nations in the face of the pandemic because we did not align our vision with meaningful preparation for this global threat. Vision is definitely not enough.

If you do not have a vision, I do not mean if you do not have a job; there is hope for you. This book will benefit you. If you have a vision you are living for, congratulations, but do not rest on your oars; you are not there yet. If your vision is accomplished and you are living in self-actualization, we salute your courage. You can give birth to another vision, and the world needs you to mentor the next generation.

This book will appeal to the intellect of an individual and a nation in a time like this. Vision must not only be conceived but followed up to fruition. As policy statements are not enough, so also mere vision is not enough.

Introduction

The beauty of life is to live for something more than you.
Why does it have to be you? Why are you here?

It could never be by accident; research shows that for every sperm that eventually makes it to fertilize an egg (ovum), about millions of sperms were released. "Sperm counts vary from 20 million to 100 million sperm cells per milliliter of ejaculation. Healthy guys produce from 1.5 ml to 5 ml of semen each time they ejaculate."[3]

The competition for life starts at that point until fertilization is achieved with an ovum (egg) and a sperm, also known as a conception of what ends up becoming a human being. It started as a rat race among millions of eligible contestants. While many germ cells become weak and cannot continue or make the journey, some flagella will be ligated through the competition. Being born to this world proves that the creator has intentions for your final emergence, making you the only one that made it among several million with an equal chance.

It is a privilege to be born and to be alive. You will do yourself and your next generation a great favor by paying attention to these facts and intentionally discover what is in the mind of God, the creator of your life. Or what are the purposes He has in mind for your creation?

What I know is that you are not a biological accident. You are not a product of evolution that goes through a metamorphosis from tadpoles or apes. Tadpole develops to a frog, maggot grows to become flies, and the human embryo develops to a human being.

You are intentionally created for a definite purpose; you are fearfully and wonderfully made. You have a trademark or DNA of the creator on you, and you are here on assignment. You are the only one wired to accomplish such an assignment; it is when you have failed or ignored the task that a replacement will be selected to accomplish the purpose you never identified, neglected, abandoned, or never achieved.

Your real profit in life is determined by the accomplishment of your purpose because profit follows purpose. The purpose must be identified and pursued to a reasonable conclusion before your announcement.

Your provision will come in the place of your assignment. You are more than this, more than what men call you, more than your job, and more than your title. You respond to the title, and it may make you happy or sad. You will agree with me that your title changes over time, depending on where you work and your performance at work. These are human devices to put labels on you. Your title may constrain your potential if you only see yourself in the spectrum of what you are trained or hired to do.

You have innate potential you cannot imagine. It is your responsibility to take yourself through the journey of discovery. Get ready to fail and prepare for disappointments, but that will be the secret to your capacity building and utilization to enhance your productivity. God and men will only pay you for the service you provide.

As you continue reading this book, you will discover that you are an important part of the human puzzle; you must identify your place and be in that specific place for the puzzle to be meaningfully completed. I will take the time to discuss vision as our primary subject matter in the subsequent chapters.

By saying vision is not enough, I am not limiting or minimizing the power and importance of vision. You must have the vision before you can run with it. More than just having the vision, some necessities must be in place for your vision to become a living and transmissible vision for others to embrace and invariably outlive your generation.

The Big Picture: Purpose

The place of purpose is in your big picture. What is the purpose? Many definitions have been proffered to this vital question by bright minds, academia, spiritual leaders, life coaches, motivational mentors, and others from different walks of life. Let us quickly look at what the leaders in various industries say.

John Maxwell describes purpose as the "ability to find ourselves, and once we find ourselves, we will find our purpose."[4] My question is, how do you find yourself when you do not know yourself? How do you know yourself when you do not understand yourself? Unfortunately, many people will never find themselves; and if you cannot find yourself, you will never give yourself to a higher purpose that you are created to achieve.

Rick Warren states that "the easiest way to discover the purpose of an invention is to ask its creator. The same is valid for discovering yourself or your life's purpose—Ask God. It is not about you. The purpose of your life is far greater than your personal ambition, desires, or happiness. It is far greater than your family, career, or wildest dreams and goals. If you want to know why you were placed on this planet, you must begin with God. You made it here by His purpose and for His purpose."[5]

In *Wake Up Your Why*, Geoff Reese says: "We are born with a purpose, a specific mission to accomplish, we are all born with a seed of genius meant to impact the world. You either become what you were created to be, seeing the reality of your purpose and contribution to the world, or you ponder them as missed opportunities at life's end."[6]

Late Dr. Myles Munroe has this to say about purpose, "the greatest tragedy in life is not death; the greatest tragedy in life is a life without a purpose. A dead man is no longer accountable for why he is not breathing, but you who are living must give account."[7] I respect the opinion of Dr. Munroe referenced above, but in my view, there is no life without a purpose. There is no vacuum in nature. If you are not fulfilling your divine purpose, you may be fulfilling another purpose. The problem is that many people will not live or fulfill their divine purpose and mandate, maybe they do not know. We all have a purpose; its fulfillment is a function of whether we discover it or we simply roll with the tides.

God's greatest desire is for us to discover our purpose for living. Proverbs 19:21 (ESV) states it this way, "Many are the plans in the mind of a man, but it is the purpose of the Lord that will stand." To my understanding, this verse implies the following.

1. The almighty God is intentional and has a planned purpose in mind that supersede human plans.
2. He allowed man to be a man; to have several plans because of man's creative abilities deposited in him at the beginning.
3. Plans should be derivative of purpose.
4. His purpose is the only one that stands, not man's purpose, family, or community purpose.
5. The purpose must be identified before plans are built around the defined purpose.

God desires that our plans for life, ideas, dreams, desired career, business, and what we want to study in college should come after discovering His purpose for our life. Matthew tells us, "seek ye first the kingdom of God, and His righteousness, and these things shall be added unto you" (Matthew 6:33, KJV). In other words, God's desire is for us to know him through relationship. From our relationship with Him, we will discover His plan and purpose for our lives.

Purpose Defined

Purpose[8], according to the oxford dictionary definition, is:

1. The original intention for anything that was made or created.
2. The reason why a thing was made or exist.
3. The cause for creation.

The purpose is the reason why a thing exists, it is the desired result for a thing's existence, and it is the source of destiny. Purpose in the writer's mind is the original intention for the cause of action. The why of a product, however, can only be answered by the maker of a product. It is the mission of a vision. Every product or service is created to meet a specific need. I have never seen anyone that created a product without an intention.

In the same way, it is evident that you are here for a bigger and higher reason than what you think or may have in mind. Sometimes our environment or background may dictate our purpose, but it is more than that. You are as unique as your purpose, as strong as a marriage bond is, your purpose is unique to you and different from your husband or wife. Identical twins that share the same uterus have different purposes in life. The discovery of your purpose in life is your personal responsibility, and you must ask the Maker why you are made or His intention for space you are occupying. It is essential to know that God is longing to discuss your purpose with you.

"I will guide you along the best pathway for your life. I will advise you and watch over you."

—Psalm 32:8 (NLT)

It is comforting to know that amidst the many paths the human heart is wired to follow that we have a Maker that never offers vain promises and never fails to guide us. It is up to you to ask Him rather than your spouse, friends, or even your pastor for guidance. God may use human agents to communicate your purpose to you based on His sovereignty, but they will constitute mere conduits for transmission.

How do you fulfill the purpose you do not know? The purpose must be known before it becomes the driving force of any life. Where it is not known, people live for alternatives, nothing, or live for anything. Every place will be a safe place; every offer will be worth trying. If you are not living for something, dying for anything will be inevitable.

How do you find your purpose? What are your passions? What are your gifts? What are you good at? Your purpose may be embedded in the purpose of another. Many will only discover their purpose by helping another man's purpose. You must serve or work with a purpose—not making it your end, but a means to an end. When a purpose is bigger than you, it becomes a calling that you live for and will ask other people to join you to fulfill. They will be your complement, not your competitors.

Difference Between Sight and Vision

"As a man sees or ears, so is he" (Proverbs 23:7).

Think about this.

We have orifices in our body that serves as a gateway through which we interact and connect with our immediate environment. All body organs are essential as they perform unique functions that bring the human body to homeostasis. My focus will be on the importance of eyes (vision) in personal, mental, spiritual, and material development. Eyes and ears are strategically positioned, and the information they capture goes a long way in the determinant of who you are or who you will become.

Let us take a quick look at the eyes and image formation from basic biology. The lens focuses light through the vitreous humor, the retina receives the image, and this image is transformed into electrical impulses that are transferred by the optic nerves to the brain. Scientists agreed that brain information processing at the subconscious level is sixty bits per second. The brain interprets the message and sends it to the mind, which can handle 400 million bits of information per second at the conscious level.[9] The image captured by the eyes become meaningful and useful for decision making. Formation of image, thoughts, action, and reaction takes microseconds.

Reagan and Noa described vision this way: "Vision is a mode of exploration of the world that is mediated by knowledge, on the part of the perceiver, of what we call sensorimotor contingencies."[10] What can you see, how far can you see, based on the level of your perception, sensation, and the reality of your foresight? No one can limit you more than the limitation your sight places on you. Your sight informs your action and reaction. Your sight may also support or be detrimental to your vision. Unfortunately, what you can see will not only be the determinant of what you get, but it goes beyond you to your posterities. It may become their permanent possession, except diversion occurs.

How you see is important; what you see, what you hear is what your mind will work on to form your perception. It shapes your life and becomes your ideal and reality; such may invariably become your family ideals. To conclude on sight, let us take a quick look at the difference between sight and vision:

- Sight presents a clear picture of the present. Vision presents the reality in your future.
- Sight sees challenges imbedded in the object of focus. Vision seeks a solution.
- Sight focuses on the physical. Vision focuses on seeing and unseen future.
- Sight is a perception of your present. Vision is faith in your future.

Stan Ellis described the differences this way: sight sees; vision imagines. Sight sees with the eyes in your head; vision sees with the eyes in your heart. Sight is for information; vision is for the revelation. You walk paths with sight, but you determine paths with the vision.[11] "It is not about your current status, it is about what you are meant to be, the destination you must reach and the destiny you are here to fulfill."[12]

Vision! Vision!

"If a man has no purpose for living, he is not fit to live"
— Martin Luther King

Having established the importance of purpose in the equation of life, I will move to the relevance of vision in achieving your purpose. I will first discuss this concept using a biblical approach as it speaks about vision more than any other book.

Where there is no vision people perish...
—Proverbs 29:18 (KJV)

I questioned this Bible verse as a teenager growing up among many rich blind beggars on the street of Ebutte-Metta, a suburb in Lagos, Nigeria. Some of these beggars are alive and well, some have beautiful wives, mansions to their name; I know some that are living in affluence, there are kings and nobles within this Blind Beggar's Community. My ignorance and my-opic views faded away with God's illumination.

Friends, the place of vision is essential in your quest for purposeful living and all other pursuits in life. Please pay attention as I carefully describe the word vision. My definition may be limited, but let us share it.

Vision Defined

"To be ahead is to see ahead. You cannot go faster than you see."[3]

—Bishop Oyedepo

I will use the physical application to make the word simple and basic for us to understand.

After Lot had gone, the Lord said to Abraham, "Lift up your eyes and look as far as you can see in every direction—North and South, East and West. I am giving all this land, as far as you can see, to you and your descendants as a permanent possession.

—Genesis 13:14–15 (KJV)

The referenced scripture launched my life to an unlimited appropriation and maximum exploration of what God has provided to the descendants of Abraham by faith in Jesus. I am boundless; no boundary nor limitation can contain or curtail me if I can see it. I must first lift my eyes, the eyes must be lifted away from every other focus, limitations, challenging circumstances, and must look with an intention to see. My considerations must also be intentional, devoid of any eye defects that may impede the object of focus; the vision must be 20/20. I must look with the eyes of faith and see with the same eyes of faith.

As we take time to define and describe vision, I want us to remember that vision can be personal, organizational, or global. Personal vision will give birth to cut-edge industries, have a global impact, and create a great organization that is known and yet imagined. We see organizations and leading industries with vision statements. It is essential to know that personal vision precedes or gives birth to organizations and industries that we see today. Sam's Club/Walmart retail store was born from a vision of a man called Sam Walton on July 2, 1962. Jeff Bezos conceived vision of how to take commerce to another level and increase his net worth. He founded Amazon out of his vision for e-commerce and virtual store on July 5, 1994. These examples bring to light the importance of a vision that is bigger than, and outlives the vision bearer. Personal vision is the starting point that will give rise to organizations, industries, endeavors, and greatness that will transcend generations.

Vision, simply, is a clear mental image of a preferable future that can be inspired, revealed, or imagined.

Vision is the energy of progress and an integral part of actions that result in fulfilling your purpose. Vision gives meaning to life, induces inspiration, and propels action. Proverbs 29:18 (KJV) tells us, "Where there is no vision people perish." A vision not born can never be accomplished. You must see the image through your eyes of faith. It must get to your heart. Your heart must be able to accommodate, ruminate, meditate, preserve, and decipher it at the conscious level before it becomes what you speak.

You create what you see and become what you say. When you speak your vision, the power of spoken words back it up and put the elements in place to cause manifestation. The vision manifested creates and becomes the life you live. Only if you believe what you confess, swing into action, and you do not destroy your confession by doubt, unbelief, and fear.

Vision is the ability to see the future that only exists in your imagination, but so real to you that no one can talk you out of what you have seen. It propels the actions. It is the eyesight, the foresight, and insight, seeing beyond the physical. The vision also serves as a clear guide for choosing courses of action. Vision is a product of deep thinking, meditation, and imagination. Vision is the engine that drives progress. A man of vision sees what God has planned for him and take steps of faith towards its fulfillment. Vision is the source and hope of life.

Why Do You Need Vision?

You need a vision that transcends sight because it is the only key that sustains your purpose. It guarantees peace and tranquility as you complete your God-ordained assignment, and you graciously handover to the next generation basking in significance rather than mere success or happiness.

Where there is no vision, the people perished, the future is extinct, and the next generation will have nothing to sustain them. The circle of servanthood continues, the society and system dictate and limit you; and the generation's perpetual extinction will be a gradual process. This reiterates Proverb 29:18a, "Where there is no vision, people perish." Your children need means of sustenance. It is only the vision that can sustain life and human pursuit. If you are devoid of vision that will transcend you, your children and grandchildren will serve other people's vision. David's vision was the key that unlocked the greatness Solomon enjoyed.

Then the King said to the prophet Nathan, "here I am living in a house built of cedar, but God's Covenant Box is kept in a tent", Nathan answered, "do whatever you have in your mind, because the LORD is with you."

—2 Samuel 7:2-3

Following on the accomplishment and preparation of his father's vision, Solomon was proud to announce to Hiram,

"You know that because of the constant wars my father David had to fight against the enemy countries all around him, he could not build the temple for the worship of the Lord his God until the Lord had given him victory over all his enemies. But now the Lord has given me rest all around since I have neither foreign adversaries nor domestic crises."

—1 Kings 5:2-4 (ISV)

What a great appreciation to a great dad. "I have rest on every side because David my father has fought all the battles" (see 1 Kings 5). What will your children say after your departure?

How Do You Give Birth to Vision?

"Your thought gives birth to your vision, and vision gives birth to the reality you live."

—Ope Adenuga

It is vital to seek the face of the Lord.

I will climb up to my watchtower and stand at my guard post. There I will wait to see what the Lord says to me when I am corrected. Then the Lord said to me, write the vision down and make it plain on tablets that he may run who reads it. For the vision is yet for an appointed time, but at the end, it shall speak and will not lie. Though it tarries, wait for it, because it will surely come, it will not tarry.

—Habakkuk 2:1-3 (NKJV)

Look at the Lord's response. When there is readiness of heart, the word of God will come. He is always with us, but we cannot see or hear Him because we are clouded with noise and cumbersomeness that takes us nowhere. The theologians will look at the context of the above discussion between Habakkuk and God as a direct message to him based on his prevailing situation and circumstances. But I want us to look at the application of this scripture and adapt to our personal life.

The place of being alone with God cannot be minimized. Divine ideas and insight hardly occur in a noisy mind or a marketplace. Intentional presence, separation from distraction that occupy and becloud the human mind must be laid aside and interruption minimized. In the place of expectation and meditation in His presence, a dialogue ensues, and illumination occurs. I will stand, not sit upon my watch. I will be attentive, focus, and desire Him in the secret place, the place of fellowship.

The preparation of the heart belong to man, but the answer of the tongue is from the Lord.
—Proverbs 16:1 (NKJV)

I will stand upon my watch, set me upon the Tower, I will watch and see what He will say unto me.
—Proverbs 16:1 (KJV)

There must be self-awareness and desire to get to the next level. "Self-awareness is the essential building block in understanding self, its limitation, and opportunities. It is the thinking skill that focusses on one's ability to accurately judge one and its environment, performance, and behavior and to respond appropriately."[14] It is a personal discovery without any external influence.

One day, the group of prophets came to Elisha and told him, "As you can see, this place where we meet with you is too small. Let's go down to the Jordan River, where there are plenty of logs. There we can build a new place for us to meet. All right, he told them, go ahead."

—2 Kings 6:1-2 (NLT)

The decision to enlarge the space they occupied was based on the assessment of the sons of the prophet. The vision for enlargement must originate from you, if not, no strength of persuasion will be strong enough to convince you that you are limited. You must be able to see it. If it is still bearable and accommodating, or you still manage to get by, there may not be any need to do something about it. If you do not see any need to do something different toward living a more meaningful life of vision, even when there is a clear vision, you will minimize and trivialize it as a fluke. The best of friends that share visions with you or encourage you to do something about your life will be tagged "arrogant, showoffs, and judgmental." With self-awareness comes the desire to do something about your present situation or predicament. This should be based on your purpose, the vision you can see. Not according to what is acceptable in your environment or among your circle of influence. There is a tendency for comfort to undermine your progress and potential; humans conform to the familiar, comfortable, and become complacent.

By helping and supporting other people's vision.

"So the advice was good in the eyes of Pharaoh and in the eyes of all his servants. And Pharaoh said to his servants, "Can we find such a one as this, a man in whom is the Spirit of God?" Then Pharaoh said to Joseph, "Inasmuch as God has shown you all this, there is no one as discerning and wise as you. You shall be over my house, and all my people shall be ruled according to your word; only in regard to the throne will I be greater than you."

—Genesis 41:37-40 (NKJV)

The vision of premiership was not developed in the prison where Joseph has seen the worst of days. Despite his predicaments, he was willing to support and strengthen fellow prisoners. Joseph was willing and ready to use his gift of interpretation of dreams in the prison for him to be known that he has a unique gift. If you cannot serve and help others, you may be short-changing yourself. The help Joseph provided to a fellow prisoner became pivotal in his progression to the prime position. Joseph had to interpret Pharaoh's dream and support his vision for him to fulfill his purpose as the deliverer of his people.

Sam Walton, the founder of Walmart Stores, was working as a team member in Kmart, founded by S.S. Kresge, incorporated in 1899. Mr. Walton offered his vision of membership retail model to his boss while he was serving in Kmart organization. Kresge was comfortable with a mere retail store, and Sam Walton proceeded with his vision to make membership of retailers. Sometimes, you may need to interpret other people's visions, serve other people before your own vision can be born. In the place of helping others, your vision will become unraveled. The question is, whose vision are you supporting as your own? If you cannot support other people in launching their vision, you may be the one delaying the birth of your vision because a selfish and self-centered soul will waste the resources of heaven.

God is a prudent owner of resources that will not allow it to be wasted. While you are working for others, you have opportunities to learn and master the skill of ownership. Show me how you are handling what belongs to others, and I will show you the missing link between you and your vision. You must write the vision down and make it plain, simple, without any ambiguity. Why? The fact that you have the vision does not mean the manifestation is immediate. Time is attached to vision; for Pharaoh, it was seven years.

Clarity and editing: Once what you hear or see is understood, the next stage is to write it down for clarity and editing. It is also an opportunity to place the vision side-by-side with God's word and make sure what you hear is in line with your purpose. Writing helps others to see and understand what you have seen that is motivating you to do what you are doing. Everybody that will identify with the vision has access to the vision they are supporting in its original form.

Faith and trust play an important role in birthing vision. Vision requires faith for fulfillment. The belief in God is essential in the first place to receive anything from Him.

But without faith, it is impossible to please God, for he that comes to him must believe that He exists and reward those who earnestly seek him.

—Hebrews 11:6 (NIV)

Your vision must anchor on faith to survive the days of small beginning and opposition. Remember, vision is the foresight into the unknown future.

In conclusion, some people's vision is drawn out by association with the vision of others, some birth their vision amid adversity, and others through experience and sufferings they go through. You must have the insight to understand the moment and identify greatness you are born to accomplish whether in ministry, business, or in academic pursuit.

Necessary Components of Living Vision

Interpretation: God is wholesome and very precise. He instructed Habakkuk to write the vision down. Why do you presume God told him to write the vision down? In my opinion, I think because the human mind is fluid and subject to forgetfulness. Some divine information needs discernment and interpretation. Pharaoh had a dream or vision in his unconscious state but was able to recollect. Recollection alone does not solve the puzzle. There was a great message locked in that dream for a whole nation that requires unraveling. Imagine if the vision was discounted. A nation would have been plunged into a disaster because of ignorant leadership. More than that, some visions need interpretation and more in-depth understanding because the things of God are spiritually discerned.

It is important to stress that you do not need to sleep before you can develop a vision; it may be a product of your imagination or inspiration. The point I am making is that visions need to be outlined, put it in an understandable form, make it specific, concise, and have the real meaning and understanding of the vision you want to pursue. If you have an idea, but you do not understand the nitty-gritty, ask for help.

Investigation:

I went on to Jerusalem, and for three days, I did not tell anyone what God had inspired me to do for Jerusalem. Then in the middle of the night I got up and went out, taking a few of my companions with me. The only animal we took was the donkey that I rode on.

—Nehemiah 2:11-13 (GNT)

Many visions are destroyed for lack of proper investigation. Many were truly inspired to do great things, many visions were clear and outstanding, but not many people embraced the wisdom Nehemiah adopted. He did personal investigations and vision analysis. Strength, Weakness, Opportunity, and Threat (SWOT) analysis was performed without any third party's opinion or input. He knew what God inspired him to do, despite the inspiration, he took time to understand the concept of his vision. He had a direct understanding of what was needed to be done. He investigated the immensity of the assignment to gain first-hand knowledge. Peradventure the concept needs to be divided and launched in phases based on available resources. He carried out a thorough investigation of the tasks he was about to take on, and the project analysis was not neglected because God inspired him. He completed his survey before holding a press conference with the team that may or may not support the vision.

Investigations will enhance effective communication of your vision to supporters and sponsors. It will also silence the pessimist because you know in-depth what you want to do. Exuberance or lack of understanding makes many people jump on what looks like God-inspired vision while ignoring the "proper planning and waiting time."

Consultation:

And the sons of the prophets said to Elisha, "See now, the place where we dwell with you is too small for us. Please, let us go to the Jordan, and let every man take a beam from there, and let us make there a place where we may dwell." So he answered, "Go."

—2 Kings 6:1-2 (NKJV)

And it came to pass in the month of Nisan, in the twentieth year of King Artaxerxes, when wine was before him, that I took the wine and gave it to the king. Now I had never been sad in his presence before. Therefore the king said to me, "Why is your face sad, since you are not sick? This is nothing but sorrow of heart." So I became dreadfully afraid, and said to the king, "May the king live forever! Why should my face not be sad, when the city, the place of my fathers' tombs, lies waste, and its gates are burned with fire?"

—Nehemiah 2:1-3 (NKJV)

There is a time to be quiet with your vision in the phase of personal investigation and time to speak out in the consultation stage. You have been talking to God and to yourself; now, it is time to talk to people that God will send your way to provide insight and information that will enhance your vision. Great visions may suffer and be aborted without proper consultation with the right consultants and kind people within and outside your circle of influence. Consulting your sphere of influence may be challenging if you are surrounded by mediocre. If you are the champion among the blind or if many people around you have eye defects (lack of insight) and cannot see clearly, you may need to look for people outside your community and circle. Look for those with 20/20 vision for counseling. Those that can see what you have seen. Real consultation will cost you; you may need to pay for what you want to know.

Offer to pay people for their time; great men and women value their time. Those who pay will always pay attention to details and will honor other people's time. Be ready to make some sacrifice to get the right information you need at the right time and in the right place. It may cost you time and money. You will never get the best of any eagle if you are not deliberate. If you are too busy to consult and seek counsel for your vision, wait till you are ready. Guess what! You will be amazed to discover that someone somewhere has the same idea you have, the same product line or same service line. Somebody will open the office for the same products or services in the space of one month while you are still thinking and procrastinating.

In 2018, I had the vision of a private medical practice that is different from the conventional doctor's office visit, but a practice where the providers will visit the patient at home and provide the necessary care. I went through all the processes required. I discussed with colleagues who will be involved in the operations and finally registered the company. While we were waiting for the credentialing to complete, two established companies with the same concepts moved from California to extend their services into the Atlanta market in January 2019. Our team was shocked to know that many people were thinking about the same product we had in mind. We are now fighting for a share of the market with other companies. You are not the sole repository of wisdom; God wants to meet the need of humanity while you are marking time and busy with other things you deem important. He can decide to use available hands, even stone.

Strategy and structure: Strategy is a synchronizing step by step approach or plans of actions. Period of strategic planning includes consulting with experienced ones, seek counsel, and gathering information. Meet with those that are doing well in that interested area of endeavor to get their quality time. The consultation makes you learn what only experience can teach and prevent reinventing the wheel. You must also determine the type of structure that will work for your vision; your vision is unique, so also must your structures.

Provisions:

I also asked for a letter to Asaph, keeper of the royal forests, instructing him to supply me with timber for the gates of the fort that guards the temple, for the city walls, and for the house I was to live in. The emperor gave me all I asked for because God was with me.

—Nehemiah 2:8

Gathering resources necessary for your vision ful-fillment calls for deliberate planning with financial or other investment projections. What will be needed for the vision actualization, and where do you get what is required? If it is money, do you have it in your bank account? Are you getting a loan from family, financial institution, or payday lenders? Will you be well off with partnership or other forms of collaboration? If it is wisdom for your ministry, what resources do you need? How do you get it? Vision can be likened to a newborn that must be nurtured with love, passion, compassion, money, time, and selfless sacrifice to succeed. This is the time to consider and have the provision in place to support the vision when needed. I was not lucky like Nehemiah that got a promissory note from the King. I could not get many friends to support some of my ideas with their time, let alone their money. Provision is essential.

Action: There is time for calculation, permutation, consultation, and also time to get on and start working. The action phase is very challenging because, in this phase, you are no more talking, but you are working. Many people will quit at this stage because it may not be what they expected; make sure you do not quit, or the vision will die. It is interesting how our team was motivated with the idea of a private medical practice, and how we work so hard, contributed money, meet periodically to assess the progress, push the credentialing, periodic consultation were done to make sure the contractors stayed on course. The first week we launched our website, the phone started ringing with requests for house calls. Some of the founding colleagues reconsidering if this is for them, they had a soul searching and evaluation of their readiness to handle a private practice. Partners quickly realized the gravity of the practice and how much demand it will have on what they consider more important. You do not have a vision until you launch your vision, and the structure you built around the vision holds it in place. The strategy and structures you put in place will be tested at the action phase.

Arise and walk through the length and breadth of the land...

—Genesis 13:17 (ESV)

Stages of Vision Development

"Expectation will set the pace for your experience. Aim nothing, hit nothing."[5]

—Bishop Oyedepo

The stages of vision development can be compared to different stages of human development from conception to birth and maturity. Some visions will not survive beyond the conception stage before they are aborted; some will go through launching and will be extinct in the first year after launch. A successful vision is the one that survives thick and thin to become fruition.

Conception Stage: I will stand upon my watch, I will see what he will say to me, this is a stage where you must write whatever you see, hear, conceive, or any mental image you develop through your imagination and meditation. Vision conception varies, but the common factor is an inspiration. Abraham was challenged to see; Joseph dreamt and saw himself becoming a prime minister. He did not lose that dream in the third stage of sleep; he woke up with it. He started confessing what he saw. Jeff Bezos imagined e-commerce with more than a billion customers all over the world from his basement. Steve Jobs believed his iPhone and products would be in every household across the globe. It is a stage of validation and consultations, expressing and exploring what it is and making sense with what seems unreal. It must be conceived and perceived before it can be born.

The Birth of a Vision: The conception of a vision to birth may take several months to several years, depending on the vision. It took Joseph about forty years for his vision to be born; imagine what he physically and emotionally went through. You are not Joseph, and I am not proposing you will go through what he went through, but there will be a lag time between conception and birth. The birth stage is the stage of manifestation of your mental image of the future you can see. It is a stage to introduce your products to the end-users. What do you offer? Why must people spend their time, money on your goods, services, or ministerial callings? What you have must be convincing and well explained at this stage. Depending on your products, be ready to use your funds or paycheck to support the baby. Bank may loan you money if your business proposal is excellent and if you have financial integrity. However, many will not support the vision that does not cost you anything.

Vision Maturity: This takes three to five years at minimum, depending on your vision, the provisions, and products. This is a stage where many visions experience challenges; this is an enormous nurturing stage. It requires your time, money, and all the support you can get and give. This is a stage you reap what you sow. If you support other people's vision, you should be bold to approach those mentors and supporters when you need advice and counsel. If your time was too precious to help others, now is the time to use the money you make to look for help. There is no vacuum in nature; what goes around comes around. If you have been greedy and self-centered all your life, it is a reaping time. In this stage, individuals tend to blame others and see enemies in others and not in themselves. This stage is challenging because you need financial and intellectual infusion to support you and the vision.

I worked as a Registered Nurse from 2010 to 2019; I never worked overtime one day even though it comes with perks and premium pay. I only worked three days a week and devoted at least two days to volunteer, work to learn, or do something to support my vision. I did not have fat paychecks like my professional colleagues, but I knew what many do not know. I do not want to build my useful years around the vision of the organization alone. I desire to be able to produce jobs one day rather than looking for a job. I worked to gain experience and gradually build the professional capacity that would enhance my vision. I think differently to avert what I have seen happen to senior colleagues that retired. After an envisaged fifty years of service and job security with these organizations, I feared my reward would be a fiftieth-anniversary certificate, Chick-fil-a lunch, and a long service award pin. It will be too late to take a risk without thinking hard on the consequence and ability to rebound if things do not work out. I am made for more than that. I saw beyond the present, some of those family vacations, sense of belonging, and approval among colleagues because we met at Las Vegas on boy's getaways; those gratifications can be delayed for my freedom.

Break-Even Point: This is the stage in which the vision moves forward or dies due to exhaustion and starvation. I have been supportive, and I cannot continue, but if the business, ministry, or endeavor make enough to take care of itself—there is hope. God must remember Joseph at this point, or he would have lost his mind.

Vision Development and Explosion: Now the vision has legs to stand on, the vision can pay its operating costs, and you have some extras. Congratulations, you made it! It is time to think about product development, expansion from in and out, creation of not for profit to reach higher goals. I love the Wellstar Health System. The vision of a world-class health system started about twenty-seven years ago in one facility; now they are almost all over Georgia within a space of time as leaders in merger and acquisition. Think about expanding your vision at this phase.

Mission

I like the description of mission by Robert Kiyosaki. "The mission is the spiritual purpose of any vision or business. The mission is what an organization is created or established to accomplish. Mission answers what you are here to accomplish, how you want to achieve it, and to whom will it benefit. If your mission is all about "I" and centered on you instead of others it has a flux. True mission is about whom you love and what you love to work for. The mission starts at your core, felt in your soul, and drives your passion for accomplishment. Passion for mission accomplishment is a combination of your love for what you do, who you serve, and the anger to provide the service no matter what it takes to get it done". Many at times, some of us know what we want to do deep inside our hearts, but the distraction and attractions around us derail the mission in our hearts. A mission will drive your vision.

What Can Prevent the Birth of Vision?

Self and Sight: The more you look away from yourself, the better you will be able to see opportunities and great ideas waiting to be discovered. The more you search on how to meet the need of others and humanity that surrounds you, the better you will find a higher calling. We are naturally wired to focus on I, me, and mine. If you only focus on yourself, all you will see is you and your family. You are the architect of how far you will go, as far as your eyes can see, no one but you will determine the extent of your greatness based on your sight and vision.

Look as far as you can see in every direction, North, South, East, and West. I am giving all this land as far as you can see to you and your descendants...

—Genesis 13:14-15

Can you beat the offer? Human selfishness narrowly thinks of what it can get and not what it can give. There must be something in it for you, or it will never get your attention nor your best if you are persuaded to volunteer. Look beyond you.

Complacency: Warren Buffet says, "I like to study failure. We want to see what has caused businesses to go bad, and the biggest thing that kills them is complacency. You want a restlessness, a feeling that somebody is always after you, but you are going to stay ahead of them."[16] It is better to hang out with people better than you. Pick out associates who have a vision and whose behavior is better than yours, and you will drift in that direction. Be aware of dream killers and those preoccupied with mundane things. We are encouraged to love all men, but relationship is a choice. Friendship is costly; a relationship is expensive. Do not discriminate, but be selective. Hang out with people that have intelligence, positive energy, and reliability. Hang out with intentionally focused people, those that know when to say "no" to almost all the unimportant things and remain focused on the few things that truly matter. If you are comfortable with friends and people that agree with you all the time, it is possible both of you will remain in the same trench for a long time.

We tend to be comfortable with our zone and those that made us comfortable. We presumed the situation will always remain the same. Joseph was comfortable with Potiphar until his situation changed; adversity pushed out the talent in him that was dormant for use. If his integrity had not been challenged, he would have remained Potiphar's personal aide, massaged and manicured his master's wife for a long time. Imagine a prime minister that has the potential to deliver a nation and liberate a generation merely surviving on leftover from Potiphar's house. Prime minister and a deliverer by ordination yet a servant and attendant. That was all he knew. The next assignment that got him in trouble was his refusal to massage the boss lady's upper torso and excite her when she offered herself.

Comfort: Most of the time, comfort is an enemy of advancement. There is a need for some level of discomfort before some of us can see a need. The sons of the prophet by themselves discovered that space is essential; it dawned on them that there was an opportunity right where they were to be more comfortable and expand (see 2 Kings 6:1-2). They thought about it, and they spoke, what you think in life is what you become, you cannot be anything better than your thoughts.

Show me a man in his true estate, and I will tell you what his thinking priorities are. They have been living in the same place for a long time, but until the reality of the limitation dawned on them and they saw the need to do something about their new desire, no one could help them. It will be a waste of good time telling pastors and prophets they are limited or living below their potentials until they realize it; no meaningful actions will be taken even if you are God sent. Human beings hate to be told what to do. You must see it before you can pursue it. You must be ready to pursue it before the Almighty God can help you despite His omniscience. The sons of the prophet are not wishful thinkers; they are not free talkers; they already have plans of actions before talking with destiny partners

Mediocrity: This is a stronghold that none of us will agree exists in our lives. It is possible to be mediocre without realizing it. Mediocrity is a state of mind. Education with its illuminating power, royal ancestry, race, familial influence, and affluence cannot limit it. Putting in minimal effort, barely getting by, not going above and beyond can cost you a lot and provides false hope that will impede vision. Take a look at Elias Kanari's seven descriptions of a mediocre. "Failure to connect with others: People will buy into the leader before they buy into the vision. Mediocrity will make you think sharing the vision is more important than sharing your good attitude. People will embrace your personality first before they embrace your vision."

If one of the following statements apply/relate to you, then you are in a state of mediocrity.

- You have stopped dreaming. Life and your service have become a routine rather than innovation and a dynamic endeavor.
- You appreciate methods than the result. It must be your way or highway, forgetting there are many methods and ways to arrive at the same destination and achieve set goals.
- You focus on what has not been done as opposed to progress made. Focus on small stuff before praising the accomplishment. It is not about what is done; it is about what is not done your way.
- You worry more about appearance than the outcome—the image rather than the result, context rather than content.
- You are always looking for a short-cut that will prevent you from learning the whole process. This may affect your better understanding of the complete concepts and prevent you from appreciating life for what it is.
- You always hit your goals without any effort: Its either the goal is too short, or the vision is too

small and can be achieved by any Tom, Dick, and Harry.[17]

People will not seek you for a solution if you are an average. There are many college professors and specialists that are mediocre. They know so much about one thing and least or nothing about many other important things of life. Unfortunately, professional attainment and appellation sometimes mask human ignorance and will prevent personal capacity development. *Mediocrity only accomplishes for self what great minds accomplish for humanity.*

Lack of understanding: It is possible not to understand the vision/mental image for the preferred future you want to live, but you must know where to turn and who to turn to in times of need. Understanding who you are and why you are here will propel the next question of what you are here to accomplish. Your purpose and how you achieve the purpose is based on your vision. He who has understanding will prepare for war at the time of peace; it depends on understanding and the vision you can see.

Laziness: King Solomon warns us a great deal about laziness (see Proverbs 6:4-11). Inability to get things done, moving slowly or sluggishly, or lack of zest. Doing the wrong thing at the right time is laziness because you will not get the right things done. Do not be surprised that some people are already living the same mental image that you have.

Lack of productivity: Productivity is a measure of efficiency, the quality, state, or fact of being able to generate, create, enhance, or bring forth goods and services. What are some attributes of productivity that may give birth to vision worth living? They include sufficient knowledge and adequate skills acquisition. Wisdom is also an indispensable commodity for productive people. Wisdom is the correct application of knowledge; wisdom feeds on knowledge, and knowledge is acquired through information, education, and experience. The proper application of the information acquired through these mediums will determine your productivity and prosperity. Understanding the dynamics of faith and applied efforts where efforts need to be disbursed with the strong belief that the effort will produce results. Productive people rise early in the morning with a purpose, and they go to bed with accomplishment behind them. Proverb 31:15 (KJV) tells us, "She rises while it is yet night and provides food for her household."

Proactive rather than reactive attitude: Being proactive means taking the initiative, it means thinking and acting ahead of anticipated events; it means using foresight, it helps in planning well for the future and averting disaster. Being reactive is tending to respond to events and situations rather than initiating or instigating them. Productive people not only see problems, but they also know the solution and plan accordingly. David identified Goliath as the problem that was terrorizing God's army; he equally saw God's ability to defeat the enemy. Saul and the army saw Goliath as a big problem to conquer and confront, but David saw Goliath as a stepping stone under God (see 1 Samuel 17:44-46). The productive people understand time is tied to opportunity, and opportunity is related to time. They use every minute to create output, they use time, talent, and treasure wisely to create increase. They do not trade time; they understand the ephemeral nature of time and know that their efficiency is measured in time, their output correlates to time.

Procrastination: Proverbs 12:27 (KJV) tells us, "The slothful man roasted not that which he took in hunting." I do not want to agree that a man that endures the jungle and the risks of wild animals to hunt and kill an animal as a reward of his enterprise is lazy. It takes a lot of courage to go hunting. I can say that he is a bad finisher; procrastination is a disease that makes one exert efforts to pursue a vision, and before anything comes out of it, the zest to conclude is gone. Procrastination wastes efforts and resources. People that procrastinate lack focus and are easily distracted—unfortunately, the gains of hunting decay over time.

Many have excellent business proposals in mind, might have done some investigation, but once procrastination sets in, the next step will not be completed until they are off course. A wasted time for one person opens a golden opportunity for others that are looking for the opportunity to become relevant. Humans will search for the place they are supposed to be and wonder why they are not in such a position once the opportunity is gone. For many, it will be too late because the clock of life is winding down. Do not procrastinate with a vision; you need a roadmap to guide you. Do not rise and go to bed, chasing the wind, being busy with no significant progress.

Many other reasons can prevent the birth of a vision: past failures, discouragement, disappointment, and many more. Nothing should stop you from the vision you have for your life because many destinies and purposes are attached to your vision. If you fail, they fail by default for no reason of their own.

The Important Question You Must Answer

"Vision is not automatically equal distinction. Men of proper action become men of distinction."[8]
—Bishop Oyedepo.

The big questions most people ask are:

- How do I know my purpose?
- How do I know I am pursuing my vision?
- How do I know what God wants me to do?

The questions you need to ask yourself are:

- Who do you want to be?
- What is your passion?
- What are your gifts?

- How will your life be impacted if your current job let you go?
- Do you have job satisfaction, or you only have job security?
- What motivates your job satisfaction?
- Do you or your family own the job, or was it offered to you?
- Where do you want to see yourself in a given time in the future?
- What landmark or legacy do you want to leave on the sand of time?
- What makes you happy?
- What is success to you; what is the significance?
- How do you want to achieve significance in your lifetime?
- What do you want to achieve? How do you want to contribute and be a part of the solution to the challenges that plague humanity?

It must be different and unique than what everybody is living for. A vision is more prominent than what anybody and everybody can achieve. One bigger than, "I want to get married, buy a new home, buy a car, a family vacation in Hawaii with my siblings, have a boy or girl." Methuselah achieved all these, yet he lived for nothing. After all, what next? Does your emptiness evaporate? In answering some of the questions posed above, there is the need to look intentionally, look inward, and find what is unique about you and what you can do better than anybody. That may be the beginning of discovery.

Let us take time to explore your uniqueness as an individual blessed by God with all you need to help humanity and your generation. It is already in your hand. What is in your hand?

What is in Your Hand?

What you have in your hand is more than enough for your purpose only if you can see it.

The Lord said to him, "What is that in your hand?" He said a staff (rod). And He said throw it on the ground, so he threw it on the ground and it became a serpent, and Moses ran from it.
—Exodus 4:2-3 (ESV)

The scripture associated with this question transformed my life in a way I cannot perfectly express. During the 2006 economic depression that started in the United States of America, with the collapse of the real estate market, Wall Street, and bank failures, the unemployment rate was high, many people were losing their jobs, and many homes were going through foreclosure. It was apparent that help must come from somewhere better than Washington D.C. because the federal government doled out stimulus packages. Still, it refused to stimulate the economy, and unemployment was at double-digit. The church was not immune to the economic disaster. I was looking for ways to encourage the segment of the church I was leading in Sunday school, and I stumbled on this scripture. It was as if I have never seen or read it before. The Holy Spirit illuminated my heart, and this has become my revival scripture because it changed my perspective.

Moses had fled Egypt for fear of reprisal; once his acts of killing an Egyptian became public, he ran for his life and became a servant tending the sheep of Jethro. He was out with the sheep outskirt the city, and he saw the burning bush that culminated in his encounter with Yahweh of Israel. God gave him an assignment and sent him back to Egypt, where he fled to face a notable king Pharaoh that may be looking for him. The fear and terror of his past were on one side, but more than that was the assignment to be God's ambassador that will liberate the children of Israel from slavery in Egypt. That was not the desired job for a fugitive and stutterer like Moses, who has no respect from this group. Moses was not hiding from his limitations; he recognized and identified them and used them as excuses for his inability. The way God caught the attention of Moses and the direct encounter and discussions that ensued made it difficult for Moses to refuse even though he gave many reasons why he was not qualified. I see God proved to Moses, "I did not look for those that are qualified, I qualify whoever I want and equip them with provisions for the assignment."

Moses, unaware that God has deposited in him all that pertains to life and godliness, asked God for validation to make Pharaoh and the people believe him. *I can see your acts; I never see you,* Moses would have thought. The response was straightforward, then the Lord asked Moses, "What is that in your hand?" I see the humanity in Moses; he knows that he has a rod in his hand, and he knows what he used it for, but he never imagined that the same "useless rod" is more than a rod. He never could fathom the same is dynamite until God asked him to throw it down on the ground, and the miracle started. The same rod has been with Moses forever; after that encounter, the rod of Moses never remained the same. The rod became the tool of deliverance for God's people, the rod that parted the red sea. This rod swallowed other rods, instilled boldness and confidence in the carrier, and was instrumental in the journey through the wilderness. Moses became famous as much as his rod.

The first question is, "what do you have in your hand?" What do you have in you that you are aware or unaware exists?" It may be a "useless rod." It may be a gift, talent, ability, or skill. All I know and convinced is that you do not need to look too hard to discover your purpose or vision; it is among the package that you came with. The earlier you identify what you have in your hand, the better and quicker you will move towards your purpose because it is instrumental in your journey. No one is born empty; everybody has something, make sure you discover it and use it to benefit humanity before your time here on earth is complete. He will undoubtedly ask you what you did with it.

Let us take a look at the instruction after God asked the question what was in his hand, he discovered and realized he had a rod that had been with him as a shepherd. I wonder why the instruction, "Throw it down on the ground..." was explicit. "Most assuredly, I say to you, unless a grain of wheat falls into the ground and dies, it remains alone, but if it dies, it produces much grain" John 12:24 (NKJV). It must touch the ground before growth, multiplication, and harvest happens. *Maybe many of us who realize that something is in our hands are not willing to release it to Him.*

It is hard sometimes to travel from the known to the unknown. Still, Moses must throw his rod down for it to become a serpent, a grain of wheat must fall into the ground for it to produce corncob, those gifting's, talents, and abilities must be released to Him in the place of service before they can come back to bless you the courier. Be ready to release them because they are too small to take you to greatness, but if you release them for God, He is able to transform them, use them for His purpose, and return them to you as the key to your solution.

In your quest for purpose and search for vision, ask yourself this critical question and answer this important question, "what is in my hand?" The discovery of what is in your hand will guide you towards a purpose you are made to accomplish and vision you are created to pursue. The next question is, am I ready to release it to wherever God wants to use it? Here, self must be compromised, insecurity must be denied, or you will fail the stage of release.

If you hold unto it, it may not do you any good, since it has been with you all this while, what difference has it made to your life? Your life has been indifferent, "self" seldom thinks if you release it, it is gone. But if you release it to His service and let Him use it the way He wants, it will initially look as if it is gone. Whatever you release to Him is not gone, it is an investment into your future. The dispossession of what belongs to you is temporary. You will surely get it back in a way that will amaze your world.

Time and space will not permit much elaboration on this truth but remember the widow, the wife of a prophet who died and left debt for the family (see 2 Kings 4:1-4). The creditors were ready to enslave the children, and she came out crying for help; the simple response from Elijah resonated with me "what do you have" the answer was "nothing except a small jar of olive oil." The poor widow has nothing left except what is incognito, little leftover olive oil, that proves to me that no one is absolutely poor or lacks an asset that can be used for their transformation only if they: Consciously and intentionally look inward and outward at the total person and the endowment that surrounds them.

No one is poor except the one that lacks the mental capacity to utilize what they have to bring about what they do not have. The realization that no one is empty and devoid of resources needed for miracle and transformation is important. Despite the emptiness and penury, there will always be something left.

The lepers in 2 Kings were an outcast because of their disease; they were abandoned, homeless, and had "nothing left" except sanity; they had the ability to think, company, and courage that conquered fear. That was all they had. They released it only to become a celebrity, and they fed a nation in desperation for food (see 2 Kings 7). Farmers understand these principles, and they experience a bountiful harvest, great investors understand this principle and build wealth. What you let go of your hand is merely leaving your hand, but it is not leaving your life. It must leave your hand before it can impact your future and bless your generation.

Since it is nothing, it is not enough, and I must let it go—How much sense does it make? Not at all, but that level of foolishness is what you need to experience the wonder called more than enough. Human greed must be challenged on the altar of release to experience a new dimension. You have everything you need to move to the next level. The resources for your vision and its accomplishment is already in you only if you can see and trust the process; the mission will be accomplished.

Early 2019, I was excited as a Sunday school teacher after being led to do some exposition on vision within my church group. Many people were interested in the study. The session was supposed to last for a month, but it lasted for about three months. Many participants asked questions about how to birth a vision and how to sustain a vision. As a teacher, I felt some level of accomplishment because we answered most of the questions proffered.

My accomplishment was pivoted around the fact that at least some people believe and can see beyond the present and take a glimpse into the future though it is unknown but only with the eyes of faith. I was energized and devoted more time to my vision. Towards the end of 2019, I had a personal experience that informed and caused a reevaluation of my recent accomplishment. I realized from my experience that having a desire to be great or having a laudable vision to live on is not enough.

I realized that having a great vision is the beginning of the journey contrary to my naïve understanding of this concept. As well as, my desire to congratulate myself as the local champion that had some level of vision among my local community; what I experienced and discovered enlightened me. I had to go back to the drawing board to reeducate my audience about my discoveries through personal experience and the experiences of others. It is important to note that the list of what you need to add to your vision cannot be exhausted only through this book. My goal is to create awareness so that we will not be complacent once we give birth to our vision and think that is all we need to do.

Vision is Not Enough

Terah took his son Abraham, his grandson Lot, who was the son of Haran, and his daughter in- law Sarai, Abram's wife, and with them, he left the city of Ur in Babylonia to go to the land of Canaan. They traveled as far as Haran and settled there. Terah died there at the age of two hundred and five.

—Genesis 11:31-32 (GNB)

This scripture gave me a better perception and motivation to write this book to help correct and inform myself and others the need for more than vision. There are essential variables needed for vision accomplishment. I have listened and read the call of Abraham and the journey of Abraham to Canaan, the supposedly "promised land" as a child. I have been sermonized all my life by eloquent pastors about Abraham's call, but I did not know that the concept of Canaan did not start from Abraham, the father of faith. The vision of Canaan, as we see in the quoted scripture, was conceived by Terah, the father of Abraham. We did not know what informed his decision. We are not told the inclination or impression he was responding to, but what we read is that as the head of his family, he gathered all his children, daughters-in-law, and informed them of his desire to relocate to a named city called Canaan.

I was wondering how Terah had a good hold of his extended family that none of his grown children above eighteen years felt otherwise or decided they were not moving with him. It is possible to attribute the family congruency to culture in the Middle East. Without wasting too much time on the family dynamics, Terah did not only have the desire to relocate to Canaan; he embarked on that journey.

Terah defeated the fear of the unknown, the anxiety of a new way of life, the challenges of starting anew that held many of us stagnant. He was not just thinking about it. He was not merely discussing it; it is no more a wish shared in the family forum. He gathered everybody and started on his journey to a new land called Canaan. The vision motivated him enough to start on the journey, but for one reason or the other, Terah arrived in Haran and settled there until he died at a ripe age, two hundred and five. The questions I wish to ask Terah would be the following:

- You announced to everyone in the family we are moving to Canaan. Why do you stop and settle in Haran?
- Where does the concept of Canaan come from in the first place? Is it a feeling, a hunch, a desire for discovery, an inspiration, impression, or a decision to change location from nowhere?
- Why did you choose Canaan out of many surrounding cities as the next city to settle?
- What makes Haran attractive to you that you decided to forget the vision of Canaan?
- In case Terah forgets where he set out to take the family, why did none of the members of the family remind grandpa that we are not in Canaan yet, when do we continue the journey to Canaan after taking a break?
- Does Terah know that Canaan was flowing with milk and honey?
- Why did he stop short of such a city?

In the city of Canaan, Terah had the vision of settling, the same city God called Abraham to relocate after Terah passed on without accomplishing his vision. Little did Terah know that if he had completed the journey and accomplished the vision he set for himself, he would have given his sons better leverage and a good start in life, not just settling as an immigrant but a landowner in Canaan.

This account made me adapt the stories to our generation's challenges and the struggles to achieve greatness. I discovered that human stories are the same, and the human mind works in the same way. For the fact that I gave birth to a vision, or I set out to accomplish a vision does not mean that I will accomplish it. I need more than vision; I need the tenacity, consistency, determination, discipline, courage, focus, attitude, and emotional intelligence to accomplish any vision I set for myself. Is it a vision I set for my business, my life, family, or vision in my ministry as church leaders? You must lead the vision and lead to the end before the vision can be fulfilled.

I would like to share my personal story with you that convinced me that this endeavor was worth the effort. In the summer of 2017, I decided to embark on providing vocational training to healthcare entry level students with my business partner. We decided to embark on providing certified nurse assistant training, the student trained would also provide the workforce for homecare agencies.

We were in Cartersville, Georgia, looking for a suitable site for the school. I shared an idea I had been thinking about providing primary care in the comfort of people's homes, as I stated in the first part of the book.

These were the days when people spend a minimum of one hour in the doctor's office for less than twenty minutes of consultation when they finally make it to the examination room. I shared this idea with four people present at the meeting, and we all agreed it is a beautiful concept. We planned to get to work with these new ideas and delegated responsibilities. My responsibility was to find an MD that will collaborate with nurse practitioners to meet the Georgia composite board requirement for Nurse practitioners to operate and provide primary medical care in the State of Georgia. I looked around as I am aware most medical doctors are comfortable, and their quest is job security. I was fortunate to find a longtime friend that was thinking about professional freedom rather than job security.

We set the process in place as partners of a private medical practice with limited liability status (LLC). We contributed personal funds to start the business; we applied for credentialing for Medicare and other insurance. About a year after the conception, a limited liability company, was registered and became operational. The vision of private primary medical care for the population that will benefit from the service was accomplished.

We were amazed at the market response even though we were not ready to be fully operational because of logistics. We started providing skeletal services as phone calls were coming. I was shocked when the reality of ownership started to dawn on my partners. Issues of life happened, and partners could not continue with the partnership despite the time, money, and efforts they have contributed in forming the practice. Folks went back to their full time employment...maybe the timing was not right. Personal responsibilities, burden of ownership, family commitments, funds, or priorities of life challenged our resolution and the vision we desire and set out to accomplish. While we are going through this shift, our competitor raised $70 million to expand the market share in the same market.

This experience and lesson from Terah challenged my curiosity, and I convinced myself based on my experience that there must be more to vision. Having vision is good, but it is the beginning of the journey. Vision is not enough because there are other determinants that makes a vision successful or fail. These variables may not be visible for others to see, but they make or mar any vision.

Vision is not enough.

As eyes are essential for seeing, so also a vision is important for the progress and fulfillment of human purpose. Mere sight is not enough, as we see in the previous chapters. For the fact that you have a laudable vision, you set out on a mission to accomplish your vision does not mean you will get to the place of accomplishment. We often sometimes believe that most people do not have vision, but the correct approach is that many people do have vision, but the vision dies halfway, or it is abandoned by the vision bearer while they moved on to something else. We discovered Terah did not make it to Canaan; he lived in Haran for more than one hundred years celebrating birthdays, anniversaries, and being celebrated until he died at the age of two hundred and five in Haran with the vision of Canaan in his mind.

What Do You Need to Add to the Vision?

The most important attributes that must be added to visions is virtue. What is virtue? Virtue is having moral excellence in character, and character is a distinctive quality and a distinguished attribute. For the fact that you have education, abilities, talents, that is required to succeed in a trade, ministerial calling, or endeavor does not mean you will succeed. It is not about what you can or cannot do, but the ability to add excellence and diligence to your allure is the hallmark of virtue. Great visions and dreams will go through challenges and tests, but visions with virtues will determine success or failure. I love the precious book called the Bible; it devoted some portion to this topic. Peter urged his listeners, who may want to be arrogant, based on the finished work of Christ on the cross. He reiterated, "For this very reason, make every effort to add to your faith, virtue, knowledge, self-control, perseverance, godliness, kindness, love." If you possess these qualities, you are confident of effectiveness and high productivity (see 2 Peter 1:5 NIV).

Virtue is a golden globe that no one can take for granted, no matter your religion or relationship. It is sad to see many people with great vision without moral excellence. Our world is full of athletes and celebrities with great talents, but their talent is extinguished in no time. Ultimately, the vision destroyed for lack of virtue. How do these attributes relate to vision accomplishment? These attributes enhance your effectiveness and tenacity to face the storm that will confront the vision. Virtue provides the moral compass that will guide the vision and what the business will be known for; fortitude and consistency

Knowledge: Have you seen many that think the birth of a vision is the end of learning rather than the beginning of discovery? They developed a vision and stopped developing themselves. Knowledge is the facts, information, and skills acquired through experience, education, whether formal or informal, the theoretical or practical understanding of art or subject.[19] Mere acquisition of knowledge is useless without application. Knowledge is not marketable; it is the skill that you market; skill is not a function of the degree after your name or the paper certificate. It is a derivative of the tactics, the strategies; you engage in handling your assignment. What is the difference between knowledge and learning? Robert Kiyosaki put it in a better way when he said, "Learning is the act of applying acquired knowledge and creating connections in your brain. Acquiring knowledge is the storage of information. When you foster self-reflection, curiosity, and imagination, you force yourself to learn. You learn about yourself, your peers, and the world around you. You question popular belief and seek your own answers, creating connections in your brain. This is learning."[20]

Mere information acquisition without application to affect attitude and practice does not benefit anyone. You must commit to long term learning for your vision to prosper.

Self-Control: We will discuss this attribute more as part of emotional intelligence, but suffice to define the word as it relates to a vision. I am very impatient, my DISC personality analysis categorizes me as Dominant, and my behavior and the way I connect with others fit that spectrum. The ability to check yourself and control your emotions, desires, or expression of feeling and refusal to react when triggered by external forces is self-control. It is a struggle for many of us.

Perseverance: Perseverance and consistency hang onto the vision when others find legitimate reasons to quit or abandon the vision. The vision you see keep the life worth living until it comes to fruition. Giving birth to vision may be exciting and frustrating. After having vision, the journey to vision accomplishment need the vision bearer to be prepared and persevering because the vision will be tested, Joseph had beautiful dreams of people bowing down to him. Still, he never saw himself being sold as a slave or be in jail in the dreams. For the vision to be accomplished, he went through a period of character building and challenges that only the strength of perseverance can overcome. Vision is not enough; vision needs perseverance and ability to hold unto it when others abandon it.

Godliness and Love: God is the author of every vision, dreams, or aspiration. Remember how we started; your purpose is enshrined in your DNA; you are unique, and so are your assignments and purpose in life. We need God at every step of our life, happy is a man or woman that understands this truth and partner with God in this journey of discovery. The manufacturer loves its products more than the users of the products because it carries his trademark. He promised, "I will not leave you nor abandon you" most times when it seems God is far away, He did not leave. We are the ones that drifted, and his love continually looks for us. He always wants us to live our vision and accomplish our purpose.

Interpersonal and Intrapersonal Intelligence

Howard Gardener, a developmental psychologist, and technocrats in 1983 has suggested that human beings have about nine different intelligence bits. The categories are[21]:

- *Naturalist Intelligence:* Special ability to understand living things and reading nature.
- *Spatial Intelligence:* Ability to visualize the world in 3D, develop robots, and Robocop.
- *Linguistic Intelligence:* Mastery of words and using the right words to paint a picture of what the mind imagined. Good expression abilities.
- *Bodily-Kinesthetic intelligence:* Found in great athletes, special athletics ability to coordinate the mind with the body.

- *Musical Intelligence:* Ability to understand sounds, melodies, pitch, tone, rhythm, and make sense out of music.

- *Logical-Mathematical:* Ability to understand figures, qualitative, quantitative algorithm, making a hypothesis, and proving them to make a conclusion.

- *Existential Intelligence:* Answer the question of human existence, why we live, and why we die.

- *Interpersonal Intelligence:* Ability to relate with others, sensing people's feelings and motives.

- *Intrapersonal Intelligence:* Understanding oneself, your feelings, and want.

My focus will be centered on interpersonal and intrapersonal intelligence. These two are essential and must be added to your vision in order for it to be a success.

Inter-intelligence determines your ability to relate with others and perform well socially. Social interaction determines how people will respond to you. Intra-intelligence is more important for success in every human vision or endeavor. It is the intelligence of the self, self-awareness, understanding your thoughts, feelings, emotions, and understanding its effect on others. It is the ability to be able to deal with yourself, hold yourself, control yourself, and delay yourself before gratifying yourself. It is the ability to hear yourself and listen to yourself before you mess yourself up. Intra-intelligence is also known as emotional intelligence; It helps you to understand yourself, react, and refine yourself and deal with yourself without anybody seeing the fight you have overcome in you. Intra-intelligence controls the self-voice that you hear all the time that determines your actions, reactions, and eventually your success and failure in life.

What you hear determines what you respond to and how you respond. Fear is a natural human response when safety is challenged or about to be compromised. Vision may challenge your safety and safe havens. As a human being, you are bound to react; therefore fight and flight becomes natural responses. How you respond to your fear is important.

As we discussed in the previous chapter, Moses released his rod, and the rod turned to a snake. He ran from the snake, normal human response, but was instructed to pick up the snake. How do you pick up what you run from? Because it has tendency to hurt or kill you? That is the place of intra communication/intelligence that must occur in humans, which will determine success, failure, breakthrough, or despondency, progression, or retardation. At that point, Moses swiftly needs to listen to himself, the inner voice that encourages him to go ahead and face a threat, or listen to offers the body will present as alternatives. He must conquer his fears and say no to other suggestions before he can reach out to the snake as instructed. We all know the rest of the story. That is the fear that keeps the best vision in the archives of human minds until it ends in the grave. And it is the fear that keeps the best minds as employees rather than an employer of labor. The fear that makes you hold onto what you have tightly because if you release it, you may lose it. Rather than investing in a vision or a dream, you stay off. The response that separates a successful vision from a vision that will not go anywhere.

You cannot overcome what you are not ready to confront. You cannot hold in your hand what you abandon or run away from. You must be prepared to grab what you are afraid of by disappointing your fears; only then will you discover there is a miracle in every seeming threat as long as you are ready to do what many will not do. Real safety is guaranteed by the one asking you to pick it up despite your fear only if you believe and trust the speaker.

Your defeat or success starts from you and the voice you hear inside of you. You are limited first by your voice, and what you hear before the situation and others around you define you. You listen to what you say to yourself more than what anybody says to you. Whatever they called you or the label placed on you is just a confirmation and reaffirmation of what you already called yourself. Your miracles, healings, and prosperity start from your sincerity to yourself before God reaches you. Vision is a journey to an unknown land that no one but you sees in the future.

Your Location and Allocation

Location is not everything; it is the right location that enhances destiny announcement. Your location and where you locate your vision is important: There is always the ideal site and location for any life to thrive. It is amazing how many people believe any seed can grow and thrive anywhere once you put the seed on the ground. There are conditions necessary for germination; different seeds thrive in different climate and topography. Smart franchise owners select sites, they conduct site analysis before business location or relocation.

There is a proper location for every life and vision before its expression and expansion. For Abraham, it was Canaan; for Joseph, it was Egypt. Men of Jericho had a hard story to tell before they finally figured out their location was the bane of their stagnancy. As you depend on God for your vision or as you are developing the mental image for the future you want to create and live, you must ask yourself two questions. Where (location)? Also, with whom (association)? "He who walks with wise men will be wise, but the companion of fools will be destroyed" Proverbs 13:20 (NKJV). Think about that.

It is essential to be in the right place (physical and spiritual location) with the right association for your vision to thrive. A wrong location will kill the best vision.

"They came to Bethsaida, where some people brought a blind man to Jesus and begged Jesus to touch him. Jesus took the blind man by the hand and led him out of the village. After spitting on the man's eyes, Jesus placed his hands on him and asked him, "Can you see anything?" The man looked up and said, "Yes, I can see people, but they look like trees walking about." Jesus again placed his hands on the man's eyes. This time the man looked intently, his eyesight returned, and he saw everything clearly. Jesus then sent him home with the order, "Do not go back into the village."

—Mark 8:22-26 (GNB)

The story of this man is pathetic. What can a blind man see? The lack of sight put this man in an awkward position and double jeopardy. He is disabled and he cannot compete in the arena of life. The good news is he had people around him that care enough to take him to meet with Jesus for a solution. He is blind, but not destitute of association. He is not empty; he has something, people that are willing to do the minimum. Here are my concerns based on Jesus, I know:

- Why did Jesus take him out of the city before he cured his blindness?
- Why not in Bethsaida? Jesus has unlimited, unrestricted power to heal and deliver. Location does not dictate to Him; he walked on water.
- Why must he take him out of Bethsaida?
- Why did he ask him not to return to the city?
- Do other people think they do not need help because they have sight?

These are questions I asked myself.

I discovered it is not about Jesus' incapacity to heal the blind man in Bethsaida, where they brought him to Jesus. It is about a man in the wrong location. It is about a man in a place that obscures and overshadows his vision. Even if he can see, he will not make any meaningful progress in that location. It is about a man or woman in a toxic association that does not support ingenuity and productivity. It is about a man in a place that will support his regression rather than progression. He is alive enough to be ordinary, but will never be extraordinary.

He may be making efforts and movement, but not progress. He may have ideas, but great ideas do not thrive in that location or among that association. When those that have 20/20 sight are struggling in Bethsaida, what chance does a man with blindness have? He was merely surviving but will never go beyond being alive, paying bills, and working to make ends meet except for the divine intervention. It is about a man that is wrongly placed and needs to be relocated for his unique vision to move forward. The man is in Bethsaida, his wrong location. It may be the right place for many people based on comparative socioeconomic equality in the community, but for this blind man; he needs a relocation. His great vision and destiny cannot survive in Bethsaida. Why? Because it is a cursed city, the man is not cursed the city was cursed; it is not about you or your vision, it is about the location. Jesus cursed the city:

Woe to you, Chorazin! Woe to you, Bethsaida! For if the miracles that were performed in you had been performed in Tyre and Sidon, they would have repented long ago, sitting in sackcloth and ashes.

—Luke 10:13 (NIV)

I was wondering for the sake of this man, Jesus will give Bethsaida a second chance and heal the land, but not, Bethsaida must have been in trouble like the fig tree without any fruit (see Mark 11). Jesus dealt with the man outside the city, and he warned, "Do not go back to the city." Are you in the right location? Is your vision in the right location? Is it with the right association? If you are not in the right location, your vision can never be.

Speaking about the location again, space will not allow exposition on Jericho; and Jordan that overflow all its bank all the time at the time of harvest. Jericho produces bitter water and barren land. The men of the city were wise; they identified a problem, refused to assume or gloss over. They would have just been alive in a beautiful city, and their life is not attractive. They seek for help in the right place.

Then the men of the city said to Elisha, please notice, the situation of this city is pleasant, as my lord sees; but the water is bad, and the ground barren.

—2 Kings 2:19 (NKJV)

What motivates or informs your location? How did you get to where you are? You are led by God, self, feelings, emotion, friends, or google? If it is outside God, mercy must rescue you. Many are ignorantly living in Bethsaida, managing life and in circles. The blind man was lucky mercy located him.

Your location is important.

Passion and Focus

What is the place of passion in your vision fulfillment? I love this definition from Brian Norris:

"Passion is a gift of the spirit combined with the totality of all the experiences we've lived through. It endows each of us with the power to live and communicate with unbridled enthusiasm. Passion is most evident when the mind, body, and spirit work together to create, develop, and articulate or make manifest our feelings, ideas, and most sacred values."[22]

Passion lets us overcome obstacles (both real and imagined) and see the world as a place of infinite potential. The passionate spirit looks at every occurrence and discovers the golden kernels of what can be, what should be, and what will be. Passion has its own energy -- an energy that's observable and transferable or infectious more than coronavirus.[23]

Bishop T.D Jakes has this to say about passion: "I believe that passion and purpose are connected; once you are in touch with yourself and discover your passion, God gives clues to your purpose." Passion is the energy that drives focus and makes humans restless even when minds, bodies, and spirits offer alternatives. It is the strength that keeps the light on and reassures the mind of its readiness once a man discovers its vision and purpose. Passion supports your vision and keeps the vision in the present until it is fully accomplished.

The power of focus must be added to your vision. Or, a great vision will end up becoming an illusion or like a television show. Anytime you remember the vision in your heart, it will excite you, but it does not go beyond the point of excitement. It does not add anything to you or bless others because it remains in a conception stage; only you know what you could have become. If only you can disappoint your fears and dare the giants of limitations. Focus on the impression on your heart called vision that you can see but not yet exists. Then, you will experience the unprecedented success that will liberate you and many others around you.

I am prone to distractions, and my visions have been distracted many times because I lacked focus. The problems are my distractors are not nonentities but tested business leaders and respected associates; they have succeeded in shifting my focus many times that I think I have the strength to get one thing done. Robert Kiyosaki defined Focus as:

Follow

One

Course

Until

Successful.

In Kiyosaki's words, "Successful people focus on goals that are bigger than them, and focus is power measured over time."

This is hard in a generation of accelerating technology and developmental changes at the speed of light. Products, ideas, application software, games, and many more items of distractions are churned out at a record rate more than what the millennials can grapple. In the midst of these, to follow one course until one is successful becomes challenging. Focus is the ability to stay on the course, no matter what is thrown at you in order to produce a brand that is precious and priceless. I also define focus as the ability to be fixated and glued to your vision until you turn failure to success. Opportunities abound all the time, great ideas and brilliant vision consume the heart and mind of men like never before, many are thinking. They do start something. What is lacking most of the time is the power of focus, strength, and integrity to tell the best allies this project must succeed, join me, or do not bother me.

People Matter

You need people to run the vision. A vision must be bigger and more than the vision bearer. I love Wellstar Health System, a dynamic healthcare organization with headquarter in Marietta, Georgia, where I started my nursing career in 2002. I remember during the first day of the new employee general orientation, the vision of the organization was carefully rehearsed to more than fifty new employees in the auditorium. Wellstar's vision is "To be a world-class healthcare system." We were told that we are special to make the final selection, and they need us to fulfill this vision irrespective of our job titles. I felt small as a certified nurse assistant, but the speaker makes me think that I am essential to their vision. I was told I am part of the people that matter to the organization.

Sometime in 2019, I wrote on an agency blog captioned, "You Need People." You need people, and also people need you and your vision. I do not mean you need everybody, neither do I imply that people are bad, but you must understand that acquaintances are not friends, and not all friends are partners, not everybody will be good enough for your vision. You must be discerning and selective.

People are attracted in many ways; thus, the power of relationships is important. You cannot succeed in your vision, or your vision cannot succeed without good relationships because people matter. Also, you will not accomplish a great vision with bad people with negative energy around you as your core supporters. Good relationships with people are necessary and important for your vision accomplishment and progress. They may not be your wife, husband, or family members, but they will be unique for your vision. Many great visions are destroyed by family sentiments and desire to make friends happy. For your vision to succeed, you must know how to put family and friends in their place if they are not insightful.

Team Dynamics

We have established the fact that good people are an essential part of your vision; relationships must be cultivated and nurtured to bring the best out in people that will serve your vision well. Whoever you have in your team will determine the success and failure of your vision. I draw insight from this story as I conclude this important subject. Vision is not enough. You need good people.

The Amalekites came and attacked the Israelites at Rephidim. Moses said to Joshua, pick out some men to go and fight the Amalekites tomorrow. I will stand on top of the hill holding the rod that God told me to carry. Joshua did as Moses commanded him and went out to fight the Amalekites, while Moses, Aaron, and Hur went up to the top of the mountain. As long as Moses held up his arms, the Israelites won, but when he put his arms down, the Amalekites started winning. When Moses' arms grew tired, Aaron and Hur brought a stone for him to sit on while they stood beside him and held up his arms, holding them steady until the sunset down. In this way, Joshua defeated the Amalekites. Then the Lord said to Moses, write an account of this victory so that it will be remembered...

—Exodus 17:8-16 (GNB)

Moses had the vision to fight a war with the attackers, the Amalekites, take a look at how it was executed, and learn wisdom for your enterprise. The Children of Israel are divided into four different groups:

- The Priests: Aaron, Hur, and Moses.
- The Army: Selected forces led by Joshua.
- The Elders from the twelve tribes: The men of experience who have seen the move of God among His people but are always torn between two opinions and easily distracted. They are always sympathetic towards the crowd but also follow Moses' instructions.
- The General crowd: mixed multitudes, complainers, those who are thirsty

Exposition

The referenced scripture above has an important insight that is relevant in leadership, team building, vision success, and crisis management (see Exodus 17:8-16). The story presented important information that cannot be discarded in working and relating with people towards achieving your purpose. Let us consider the story; the success of the children of Israel in the texts is not because they had water that they desired to drink. It is because men of vision established a mission and took their position in an established team under an appropriate leadership. It was evident that God gave Moses as the leader the mandate and the assignment. He had the vision, but he did not have the winning strategy. A team is a dynamic group, with each member having a unique ability to contribute to team growth. The "Moses," as a strong leader, must stay focused and prioritize. Fighting a battle is overwhelming enough, but to combine it with whiners and the requests of the mixed multitude is exhausting as well. It is important to note that you do not win a battle from the valley; you must take it to the mountain to have a vantage position. Your strength as a vision bearer determines the strength of your team and the sustainability of your vision. If you quit, the team will quit.

Based on previous experiences, I think Moses thought the war would be a quick bombardment, and Israel would win in record time. He was wrong. The battle is more than a rapid assault. Any war is unpredictable; you can never predict the challenges that will confront and attempt to destroy your vision, prepare for the worst, and be ready to stay focused to the end.

We are encouraged through the texts to think twice before you start a fight; you may not end what you started. The Amalekite attacked the army of Israel based on their army's strength without realizing the strength of the Israel army is Yahweh, the mighty God. Moses also discovered this battle is different, but it is too late to quit and too late to make some strategic adjustments. Men are dying on the front line. The only option he had was any suggestion from his team. As a leader, it is crucial to stay engaged with the team in a period of adversity.

Aaron and Hur are Moses' companions. They are men with initiative. They exercise the right judgment without being told, utilizing the available resources to support the vision and achieve success. Mind mapping is a continuous process in every business, ministry, and vision success. Moses is sitting on a stone that is a crucial part of the contingency plan to win the war. Moses had no choice but to follow his subordinates because his strategy was only good for the short term. The real fighter in this story was not ground forces led by Joshua; they had a part, do not get me wrong. Those that made it happen were Aaron, Hur, and Moses as a man of vision. Surround yourself with accelerative thinkers, dreamers, and people with common sense. It will get you far and help you successfully win crucial battles in your life.

Application to your vision:

- Your success depends on who you have as your core group, those you select to run the vision with you.
- Your vision is as good as those you engage to implement the vision.
- You are as great as who you talk to and who speaks to your life.
- Your vision will succeed or be defeated based on who you have in your team. You cannot have a good outcome when you are around the wrong company. It does not mean that people are evil. It only implies that they are not suitable for the task you have at hand or ahead.

- Build your life and vision around those with insight, foresight, and independent thinking.
- Surround your life with those that will do anything possible to make your dream succeed. God spoke to Moses, not Aaron or Hur, but they were engaged like Moses.
- Listen to your team.
- As a leader, the fact that you have the vision does not mean you have the best solution. Overcome your doubt, fears, insecurity, and listen to good people around you; it guarantees success.
- There is time to ask questions; there is time to follow the followers' directions as a leader.
- Identify the bright minds among your team and surround yourself with them. They are not your competitors but complements.
- There are no terrible followers, only bad leaders.
- Courage is not an absence of fear; it is the ability to act effectively in the face of fear, with the determination to go and still do what is essential despite the challenges that we fear.

My Last Cent

As you embark on understanding your purpose, which only your Maker knows and can unfold, you must understand the place of vision. The challenges we face are that many of us do not know or understand our vision. What you do not know you cannot pursue; that is why we spent ample time discussing vision.

When you have the vision, understand that it is the beginning of your exploration into your why. The "why" question is bigger than your professional pursuit, marital accomplishment, or economic achievement. As you discover your purpose and vision, you will find out that it is more than you; it is the core that your existence revolves around. If you do your part to unravel the mystery of your purpose, you will discover your action would have liberated many generations that will come after you. It will provide a springboard and a good foundation they can build on.

It is amazing to know that when human beings miss opportunities, they will pick up options, a replacement, and good compensatory measures to fill the void. It may be in association, work, sex, and some appropriate or inappropriate behavior to diffuse personal regret and inner tension. The alternative may even be as good as raising a family. The generation of Enoch lived an average of seven hundred years, a generation blessed with longevity. They all died ordinary men with common achievements without anything more significant than being born, raising children, and supporting their family. Nothing more to live for until Enoch broke the rank. He lived for lesser years and lived for something more than himself. He walked with God (see Genesis 5:24).

I often hear professional colleagues when they request counseling, "Business ownership is too hard, vision is not easy, all these big ideas, it is a lot of work. Many government regulations to keep up with, I cannot do it. All I want is to pay my bills and stay out of trouble." Excellent choice, but remember that if you do not own it, the owner owns you, be it an organization or corporation. Many generations after you will continue on the same path. The top one percent will be preserved, and the top ten percent will continue to own our jobs and means of livelihood.

Imagine if you have built your life around a wonderful job that has been sustaining you for twenty years. Within a week of the COVID-19 pandemic, all you received from your employer was an email that the job is gone, the virus has infected your secured job. No celebration or sent forth party for your dedication, commitment, and service to the organization. Can you see you are not as valuable to the organization as you thought or as they made it seem? Let me rephrase that you are valuable as long as the organization profits on your creativity.

Vision liberates the vision bearer and many generations that will follow. As you think about your comfort or complacency and the comfort your secured job provides, remember that "children learn what they live." The children will pick it up from where you stop serving others because you gave them no option.

David's vision was instrumental in Solomon's success; the direct impact is his prosperity and the prosperity of a great nation. A prospered nation with one hundred percent ownership, security, and cities devoid of homelessness.

During the lifetime of Solomon, all of Judah and Israel lived in peace and safety. And from Dan in the north to Beersheba in the south, each family had its own home and garden.
—1 King 4:25 (NLT)

Conclusion

Vision is the driver to your purpose.

In conclusion, I was once asked: Must everybody have a vision? Or, is vision for everybody? Must everybody own a business, whether small or big? If yes, how do businesses and organizations get people to work? My answer is everyone ought to have what they are living for, whether in ministry, business, calling, or whatever we call it. Unfortunately, many are living for nothing and exist in a circular motion. They roll with each day as it breaks. Vision is not an end in itself; it is a means to an end. Vision drives you to the destination and the future you want to create and live. Your vision is personally based on the insight, foresight, environment, background, association, strongholds, and the opportunities that surround you.

Entrepreneurship is not for everyone, as poverty and prosperity are not for everyone. It is a deliberate choice with associated circumstances. Ownership comes with a price; you must reject the immediate offer of gratification that procrastination and the visionless people will offer. You must defeat the fear of failing, work hard, do what many will say it is "too hard" to build an economy and be rewarded with freedom. You can get a short-cut to college; parents can pay off your debts. When it comes to living a life of significance, there is no short-cut. We all have a choice to make; our actions and decisions determine our outcome.

I love this instruction from the sacred book: "For the poor will never cease to be in the land" (Deuteronomy 11:15, NASB). The beauty of these words are no names were attached to the poor that will not cease in the land. I am yet to see anybody or family that goes with "poor" as the first or last name. We are all given equal opportunities to add our name to the side of the equation based on our vision and so many factors that form who we are.

When you have a vision, you must understand that vision is not enough. You must acquire knowledge, gain wisdom, develop attitudes that will support your vision, and put the essentials into practice for successful accomplishment and fulfillment of your purpose. A great vision is bigger than the vision bearer and must have the capacity to outlive generations. Be sure to live for what is more than you.

You are created to have dominion; be sure to make a difference this one life.

Learn More

As expressed in the book, my path may be different form your path. I feel obligated to share the information with you.

Please let others know about the book:

- Pick up another copy as a gift
- Recommend the book to your family, friends, book club, and reading group.
- Use it in your small group discussion.
- Share a link to the book.

Contact Details

Toll Free: 855-475-0814
Fax: 404-891-4959
Email: *info@vine21.com*
By Mail: P.O.BOX 801502, Acworth, GA 30101.
Connect with us: Kennesaw Eagles Meetup Group.
Visit us on the web at: www.vine21.com

Endnotes

1 Wolff, Edward. 2019 Edward N. Wolff (2019). Levy Economics Institute. NBER Working Paper Series. Accessed March 25, 2020. www.nber.org/papers/w24085.

2 DISC Personality Profiles. Angel Tucker. 2018. Accessed April 2019. www.personalityprofiles.org.

3 Huffington Post. Nine Things You Never Knew About Sperm. David Freeman. 2013. Accessed 2018. www.m.huffpost.com.

4 John Maxwell. 2017. "Today Matters." Equip.

5 Rick Warren. 2012. The Purpose-Driven Life. Zondervan Publishing.

6 Reese Geoff. Wake Up Your Why. 2015. www.learnoutloud.com.

7 On Leadership, Vision, Purpose and Maximizing Your Potential. Myles Munroe (2014), Accessed April 5, 2020. Retrieved from www.forbes.com.

8 Oxford Dictionaries, s.v. "purpose," accessed April 8, 2020.

9 Image Formation: MIT Technology Review. 2009, Accessed April 8, 2020. www.technologyreview.com.

10 Regan, K. and Noa, A. (2001). A Sensorimotor Account of Vision and Visual Consciousness. Behavioral and Brain Sciences. 24, 939–1031 Printed in the United States of America © 2001 Cambridge University Press 0140-525X/01. Accessed May 3, 2020.

11 Spiritual Legislation. Stan Ellis. 2020, April 5, 2020. www. spirituallegislation.com.

12 Bishop T.D. Jakes (2018). Your Passion and Your Purpose, T.D. Jakes, 2019. www.pottershouse.org.

13 Making Maximum Impact. Bishop David Oyedepo. 2000. www.domi.org.

14 Emotional Intelligence 2.0, B. Bradberry, J. Greaves. (2009) www.talentsmart.com.

15 Making Maximum Impact. Bishop David Oyedepo. Dominion Publications, 2000. www.domi.org.

16 Warren Buffet 2013 (USA TODAY). Comment at Coca Cola shareholder meeting in Atlanta, Georgia.

17 Seven Warning Signs That You Are Living a Life of Mediocrity. Elias Kanaris, February 2017. https://www. eliaskanaris.com.

18 Making Maximum Impact. Bishop David Oyedepo. Dominion Publications, 2000. www.domi.org.

19 Webster Dictionary, s.v. "knowledge," accessed April 2020.

20 Kiyosaki, Robert, (2012) Rich Dad's Before You Quit Your Job. Accessed April 2020, Retrieved from www.scribd. com.

21 American Development Psychology, Nine Types of Intelligence. Howard Gardner. 1983. Accessed March 23, 2020.

22 Brian Norris. "Do Things With Passion or Not At All." 2012. Wordpress. April 2020. 7thheaven.wordpress.com.

23 Yahoo Blogpost, 2019 Passion: The BlogPost, accessed May 2020. Retrieved from www.answer.yahoo.com.

CPSIA information can be obtained
at www.ICGtesting.com
Printed in the USA
LVHW011128171220
674417LV00003B/386

9 781647 735401